THE NATIONAL POETRY SERIES

The National Poetry Series was established in 1978 to ensure the publication of five poetry books annually through five participating publishers. Publication is funded by the Lannan Foundation; Stephen Graham; the Joyce & Seward Johnson Foundation; Juliet Lea Hillman Simonds; the Poetry Foundation; Olaf Olafsson; Mr. & Mrs. Michael Newhouse; Jennifer Rubell; The New York Community Trust; Elizabeth Christopherson; and Aristides Georgantas.

2011 Competition Winners

With Venom and Wonder, by Julianne Buchsbaum of Lawrence, KS
Chosen by Lucie Brock-Broido, to be published by Penguin Books

Your Invitation to a Modest Breakfast, by Hannah Gamble of Chicago, IL
Chosen by Bernadette Mayer, to be published by Fence Books

Green Is for World, by Juliana Leslie of Santa Cruz, CA
Chosen by Ange Mlinko, to be published by Coffee House Press

Exit, Civilian, by Idra Novey of Brooklyn, NY
Chosen by Patricia Smith, to be published by University of Georgia Press

Maybe the Saddest Thing, by Marcus Wicker of Ann Arbor, MI
Chosen by D. A. Powell, to be published by HarperCollins Publishers

MAYBE THE SADDEST THING

MAYBE THE
SADDEST THING

POEMS

MARCUS WICKER

HARPER ● PERENNIAL

NEW YORK ● LONDON ● TORONTO ● SYDNEY ● NEW DELHI ● AUCKLAND

HARPER PERENNIAL

HarperCollins books may be purchased for educational, business, or sales promotional use. For information please write: Special Markets Department, HarperCollins Publishers, 10 East 53rd Street, New York, NY 10022.

FIRST EDITION

Designed by Lisa Stokes

Library of Congress Cataloging-in-Publication Data is available upon request.

ISBN 978-0-06-219101-4

12 13 14 15 16 OV/RRD 10 9 8 7 6 5 4 3 2 1

Contents

II. Beats, Breaks & B-Sides

MAYBE THE SADDEST THING

To You

The mute boy piano
virtuoso in the deep
stone well.

That single-body
cold each day.
That, nights, he thinks

he shrieks.
That moonless dark
blotting out a mouth

hippo-wide. Hole
puncher is to paper
as who is to poem?

Easier magnifying
glass than mirror.
O, the things unseen:

enflamed epiglottis,
small busted voice
box, symphonies

scratched on stone
well lines—more
loose leaf, really,

than ledger.
This void—that boy
is or could be you—

depending on the eye.
Unless, you've never
longed—to be seen,

heard so bad. That,
nights, you cave—
cancel the self.

Say it sad and plain:
that this poem
is a void.

That this well is
as far as your voice
has ever carried.

Love Letter to Flavor Flav

We know we are beautiful. And ugly too.

—LANGSTON HUGHES

I think I love you.
How you suck fried chicken grease
off chalkboard fingers, in public!
Or walk the wrong way down an escalator
with a clock around your neck.
How you rapped about the poor
with a gold-tooth grin.
How your gold teeth spell your name.
How you love your name is beautiful.
You shout your name 100 times each day.
They say, if you repeat something enough
you can become it. I'd like to know:
Does *Flavor Flaaav!* sound ugly to you?
I think it's slightly beautiful.
I bet you love mirrors.
Tell the truth,
when you find plastic Viking horns
or clown shades staring back,
is it beauty you see?
Or Vaudeville?
To express myself honestly enough;
that, my friend, is very hard to do.
Those are Bruce Lee's words.
I mention Bruce Lee here, only
because you remind me of him.
That's a lie. But your shades do

mirror a mask he wore
as Green Hornet's trusty sidekick.
No, I'm not calling names.
Chuck D would have set cities on fire
had you let him.
You were not Public Enemy's sidekick.
You hosed down whole crowds
in loudmouth flame-retardant spit.
You did this only by repeating your name.
Flavor Flaaav! Flavor Flaaav!
I think I love you. I think I really might
mean it this time.
William. Can I call you William?
I should have asked 27 lines ago:
What have you become?
How you've lived saying nothing
save the same words each day
is a kind of freedom or beauty.
Please, tell me I'm not lying to us.

Self-Dialogue Watching Richard Pryor
Live on the Sunset Strip

What of stepping outside the door on fire?
What of running down a faceless road
Let alone a busy strip, enflamed? Got-damn!
There must be 10,000 selves in an epidermis. Imagine
Yours. Imagine the skin-peeling flame of each self-
Inflicted arson. Imagine the freedom to say God
Damn! To consider what that feels like. To speak
A wild geyser spraying from a busted hydrant.
You watch Richard Pryor in a loud fire engine
Red suit—all flashing lights, sirens: 10,000 selves
Visible to the world, & consider what that feels like.
To think, you may or may not be God damned.
To know, at least, your dick is intact.

Love Letter to RuPaul

You have one of the longest,
thickest, most veined, colossal
set of hands that I have ever seen
and, frankly, they cast a spell on me.
Not that I'm the type of man
who goes around checking out
other men's hands, but I know
tightly tucked cuticles
when I see them. Even sexier
is the hourglass-shaping choke hold
you can put on a mic.
You could hurl a two-foot monkey
wrench at a mirror
or pull out
and push in a date's chair
with the flick of a wrist.
I bet you don't though. Bet you've never
carried a man up four flights of stairs,
limp arms flailing every which way.
And if you have, I bet you took care
to cradle his neck. To avoid banisters
and to walk slowly. Because you are fierce
in the way only a 6'7"black drag queen could be.
In one of my earliest memories, you are wearing
a pink sequined dress, endorsing a hamburger
Good enough for a man. Maybe a woman.
I am a black man who has never worn pink—
not a polo to a country club. Not gators
to a church. And still, that commercial

ravished me. How hard, to be sandwiched
between what and who you are, tickled
by every cruel wind, critic-voyeur
playing rough beneath your skirt. How
raw you must be. To sit before a camera,
legs uncrossed.

Love Letter to Justin Timberlake

When I think of you
it is always of a small, locked room.
A principal's dark, full lips
pressed together in a smirk. A glare
from his fat, gold herringbone chain
burning tears in my eyes, my face
red as yours in direct sunlight. And
even as my voice shut down
that day, I knew ditching
to buy *NSYNC's CD
was worth more than
Prescriptive Speech class.
What I heard: four voices
harmonized in a plastic bottle.
Your falsetto, blowing the top off.
Michael Jackson
with no abusive boxer father
or snatched childhood.
Sam Cooke
sans German shepherds
stalking through his songs.
I've been watching James Brown
and Jackie Wilson make
pelvic fixation public domain
since I was old enough
to work a remote. And I have yet
to elude starched lines. How did you
learn to dance your way out of boxes?
Or did you

find it easy as breathing, like whistling
the national anthem?
Do you remember the Super Bowl?
How you tore Janet Jackson's breast
from her top?
I love you that way.
Her earth-brown bounty of flesh—
large, black nipple
pierced, wind chapped, hardened.
And you saying, Go ahead. Look.

Love Letter to Pam Grier

Dearest Pam,
I still dream of you.
College. Our second date.
How the ceiling fan would not cure
my fever that day, the white walls
beaded in sweat. I could have killed
my white friend for walking in on us.
Or kissed him right there in the dorms.
Damn the smoldering Newport cherry
that bathed my room in red. And you
cocking back that cold, hard Glock
against Samuel L. Jackson's dick.
My white friend and I, we could have
unzipped in front of the TV screen
and wrestled for the tube of Lubriderm.
I don't know what scared me more:
my roommate's wood or the camera,
out of breath, climbing mountains—
those muscled, brown thighs.
How were we supposed to compete
with Sam? Richard Pryor? Or Kareem?
With any man on your list of lays?
My mother's answer: *fuck foreplay*—
the other Pam's bed-tanned *Baywatch*
castmates taped to her teen son's wall.
For my thirteenth birthday she framed you
garnishing a large bed in red lingerie.
I'm sorry. I never hung your poster.
Even now I don't know how

to love you right. But I suspect I was
onto something back in middle school,
unsticking the other Pam
to make room for my present—
four walls. So blank
and unassuming.

Love Letter to Jim Kelly

When it comes, I won't even notice it.
I'll be too busy looking good.

—JIM KELLY, FROM *ENTER THE DRAGON*

See a clumped baby-fro budding below
Enter the Dragon's hyperbolic grunts
and you, unsheathing that samurai sword
from bulging, white bell-bottoms—slaying eight
flower dresses in one scene. Or strangling,
with plucked chest hairs, wide-open women cops.
Imagine: a black silk pajama shirt
blown open. A boy leering on the couch.
Now picture my mom, Delilah, with shears.
Mother sees you and thinks, *lothario*.
Will not hear that besting another man
ten-gallon-fro intact
is Western as a Marlboro Man ad.
But you know your business, Jim. I see you.

1999

We used to angle our asses off.
Like, say Cindy the flautist's
blouse was see-through. Say
she was sporting a tight *Les
Misérables* camisole underneath.
We might hit her off with an
unexpected mixtape, all show
tunes and power ballads. We might
compare the lead actors' recurring
sparks to an echo. Might use this
tidbit to tongue a girl down
in the instrument closet. After
school, fully dressed, bodies
enmeshed like two wild-eyed
ravenous stars, expressing
their nature—barrel-roll style.
Saliva-heavy kisses, lips
smacking, rattling
snare bottoms. We jockstrap
gossip tweakers. I remember
asking Ashley to Spring Fling
because I'd heard
of her oral inclination.
We took notes, memorized
what worked on who. Rico
told me Ashley liked daisies.
I appealed to her inner kid
for weeks. Chased her
around the timpani, tickled

her midriff
with a feather marching plume.
Kept it on an innocent tip.
Until she got thirsty
at the dance.
We walked past punch bowls
to the main hall, held hands
as she drank from a fountain.
She made a left
at the make-out corridor
with droopy stems
stuck to walls.
I didn't even get to kiss her
face. I didn't know Rico
had followed us. Didn't know
he would jam Ashley's
hand down his pants. That
she'd slip her other palm
down mine. I didn't even
get to say Stop. Ashley,

I've spent 50 lines, 3,892
days flattering myself. Thinking
I'd used some next-level mind
game to get you
where, no, how, I wanted you.
But you sized me up
in under a minute. Examined
the stain just left of my fly.
& then you smirked, *I knew it.*

Oblivious Spring

DETROIT, MICHIGAN

Obtuse red bolts cranked at each corner of the lot. Shirtless kids slapping hydrant-spray at largemouth-bass grins. Thin strands of water nearly blind Eastern Market cement. My wife, Jill, and I, we're in the thick of it, managing to overstep their runoff. Gum-popping teen lovers and elderly couples are weeds in aisles. Row after weedy-row they knock our hips together as we browse every pink beaded hollyhock, golden black-eyed Susan, and perky, white, perspiring snapdragon on display. We take an oblong tub of crimson clover and red poppy off a vendor's hands and I say the city is breathing. I prepare for a scene. Wait for her to miff our identical stride with a kiss and *Oh, baby! I always wanted to marry a walking poem!* Smiling, she reaches for my hand, locks her fingers for a moment, says *Yes. Yes, it sure is.*

Mint, basil, thyme, and trout pot the breeze. Jill's pinched nose and lips twisted east and west say she's unsure of the aroma. She leads us to a corner bistro, plops her purse on a menu and I order Bloody Marys, no celery. A table between us, we smile awhile, talking about the garden we haven't sown. Beneath the table, we place our feet on one another's seats when hydrant-spray starts leaking against our tub. I look down to adjust her knotted gold anklet and sigh at a hummingbird, flapping near a cigar plant, in a banged-up plastic bed. She points just below the bird. *Well would you look at that butterfly go to town on those little pistils!* Jill. Oh, Jill. The things that woman sees.

About the Time Two Ducks Advised Me on Matters of the Flesh

The weight of last night's bloody rib eye, wine, and crème soufflé has guilted us into the gym. Jill's trying to take the StairMaster's title again, sweat spilling from her brow like rain beyond the entrance window—a speed which rivals a woodpecker knocking at a telephone pole, after months spent idle in a sparse-stumped clearing. She looks left, laughs, and I can't really blame her. What she sees is me cruising a stationary bike. Moisture has found my face. It begins at a glistening thigh palmed by spandex shorts. It ends in spittle dribbled down the chin. My mind is wandering Jill's upstairs lair, tripping over bottled water lining her cupboard. I'm thinking about mud particles, decayed twigs, and demolished earthworms distilled. I'm wondering what it takes to kill a thing's root. Beyond the sidewalk, dwelling in a sea of lawn, two Pekin ducks should be charged with lewd conduct. The larger, presumably male, bounces on the skinny one's rump to the storm's steady pulse. I try to smile at Jill but she's headphones-deep in another world. The rain turns, beats harder on the gym roof. The drake's wide orange bill begins to nip at the woman's head. Lightning welts the sky and he's pecking. Jill's high-stepping something awful. Thunder shakes the window. Someone's knocking wildly at someone's skull. I stop.

Interrupting Aubade Ending in Epiphany

Could I call this poem an aubade if I wrapped it
in fragrant tissue paper? If I locked this morning

in the mind's safe-deposit box and polished it
sixty-six times per day, until a sky's description noted

the number of feathers on a sparrow's left wing
and the crabgrass jutting from his uppity beak?

I once wrote a poem about a fruit fly orgy
in a grape's belly. Its crescendoed combustion

was supposed to represent the speaker's feelings
for a wife named Joy. That poem never really

worked out. This poem is aware of its mistakes
and doesn't care. This poem wants to be a poem

so bad, it'll show you a young, smitten pair
poised in an S on a downy bed. The man inhales

the woman's sweet hair and whole fields
of honeysuckle and jasmine bloom inside him.

He inhabits a breath like an anodyne and I think
I could call this poem an aubade if it detailed

new breath departing his mouth. I think I could
get away with that. Because who knows what

that even means? Maybe I mean
that's safer than saying it straight

like, This is about the woman I'll marry.
How one summer, she hit snooze four times

each sunrise. This is about her smiling
and nodding off, and smiling, and listening

to me mumble into the back of her perfect
freckled shoulder about anything but poetry.

And this morning at my desk, in the midst
of a breath, I remember not every moment

needs naming. I know precisely what to call this.

Everything I Know About Jazz
I Learned from Kenny G

All right, so not really. But the morning my pops found Kenny G lying on my nightstand I did learn a black father can and will enter a bedroom, only to find Kenny's CD, bad perm and all, cuddled too close to his eighth-grader's head. He will tiptoe from the room, turn the knob, then kick down the door in slippers. He'll drag the boy out of bed down two flights of stairs and toss him in front of a turntable. Listen here, he says. When you finish a record put it back in the sleeve and you better not scratch my shit.

I curl into a ball on our shag brown carpet and stare at his wall of LPs. Breakfast folds into lunch before I move an inch. When supper rolls around I am shaking. (This is how jazz begins. Out of hunger.) Getting to my feet, I pull a record from the shelf, read: *Black Talk!* Charles Earland. A needle collides into an empty groove and out sweats a funky wash of organ. It feels like the afro's voice, grinning from the record sleeve, has picked itself out in my gut.

Eric Dolphy squeals, leaps, and dives inside my abdomen. Roy Ayers kneads and vibrates my chest. Freddie Hubbard's wail could crack glass, my ribs. Pharoah Sanders shivers all over my face. Every wax-gash, knick, and hiss. Every cut. Every record pierces skin. I tap. I drone. I thrash. I scream. I listen to the *Freedom Now Suite*. It sounds like a welted voice wincing at the basement's night. A voice my father hears too.

He does not cave the basement door. He walks a dirge down those steps. Gently strokes my neck. Asks, Why are you crying, son? Dad, I ache. Because I've been down here forever.

Self-Dialogue Camping at Yellowwood State Forest

Driving east on 45
Red & white pines / resemble neat rows
Of nooses / hung from navy sky / knotting
All / the oxygen surrounding your frame.
Can even one of ten friends see / you struggle
For space inside / a gutted speck of forest?
Does anyone notice / the way trees shrink
Breath inside / your tiny throat?
Someone sees / makes a joke about death
That lashes your spine / with cold / pimpled fear.
Nightfall chatters in space / between lips
& your stomach / is stuffed with white teeth.
The next morning smells of quelled fire.
The next morning sings deliverance.

To a White Friend Who Wonders Why I Don't Spend More Time Pontificating the N Word

What do you want me to say?
When I'm riding shotgun in a shiny Escalade—
black speck stuck to a frat-white interior.
When rap parts automatic windows—
becomes integration's dangerous sound track.
When every mouth in the whip but mine spits
the score's every n word–note—I get all warm
& fuzzy inside! I feel acutely American.

Remember that Sunday at the AME church?
You belted "Lift Every Voice & Sing"
like it was yours—carried the choir
when the second verse dropped. I pledged
allegiance to the background—swayed
in silence with the lively congregation.
After service, you polished off two plates
of collards, sucked neck bone marrow.
I piled on potato salad. Stuck to cottage cheese.

Do you recall how hard rain
drenched everything that night
on the curb outside of our dorm?
We passed Paul Masson while I cursed
Christy Carmichael's parents. Told you
how I'd sat in their kitchen, pretending
to admire flag-heavy furnishings. Imitated

the exact pitch of their laughs
after Christy said I was her tutor
for Early Western Civ. (I laughed then.
Now, I'm chuckling in a different hue—
shaking my head at that
crack about feeling American.)
They asked if I knew "gangbangers."
Had cousins in prison. Bullet-riddled kin.
I wept while telling you this. & you held me
until I stopped. Matt, you know the score.
You must think I'm some sort of wigger.
Wanna know if me & the word are acquainted.
Wanna know why I won't say it in front of you.
You want me to share it, old friend.
But you could never be my nigga.
You don't have what it takes.

Love Letter to Bruce Leroy

You every-single-syllable-articulating, left-his-mojo-in-the-dojo,
proper-posture-having, overzealous, no-break-dancing chump.
You unseasoned shrimp-fried, chivalrous sucka.
You pelvically challenged or something?
You Rubik's Cube.
You couldn't learn Cool if it came with an illustrated manual.
You eat soul food with chopsticks.
You black Orient. You occidental Africa.
You would rather kiss a man's Converse than sport a pair.
You thought that Cuban Link–choked, shiny-suited Harlem
Shogun came straight out of a comic book. & you were right.
You mastered the art of using a black belt as a belt.
You talk in riddles: *Search for art in everything. In fortune cookies.*
You find empty fortune cookies like life: containers
fitting for your art.
You have reached the final level: when the mind becomes the self
that guides without archetypal help.
I bet you keep LeRoi & Levis on the same bookshelf.

1998

Maybe it's the half
communion wafer
yellow moon in my eye.
Maybe it's the thug wind
mingling fragrant herb
firing shots
across a synapse
that takes me back
to summer. Outkast.
"Return of the 'G.' "
I was a bone, head
caught between middle
& high, private & public
school. Me & B.
used to run the drain
in his father's fifths of Crown.
Used to do C-sections
on Swisher Sweets, talk shit
about Rodney's chipmunk
teeth. & deep down
I must have been aching
to knock one out. Me & B.
were rocking back & forth
on plastic porch chairs
when Ypsi's no. 1 gossip
approached. Sheila said
Rodney was talking reckless
about my younger brother.
I inhaled a pulsing red fist

from the midsection, blew
smoke through bull nostrils,
knew exactly what to do.
We placed a few calls.
Told every teen on the block
they should come to the park
around noon. I grabbed
my pigskin, set teams
of five. B. snapped
a short bullet pass
to Rodney &
five guys nailed his back
to the grass; rained down
sharp laughs & elbows
to ribs. Teed off
on his groin.
I tried to drill a hole in his face.
Blasted my knuckles
against his incisors
again & again & again. &
I can't go on talking
to you this way
any longer. All this time
I've been working up
to say something about
that liminal place between
manhood & cartoon-
cool. Something stupid
like that. Rodney,
I chased you through
cul-de-sacs & lawns. Chased
you west through the state

of Michigan. & still haven't
figured out how to finish
this letter. I just want
you to know. & I understand
this is no consolation. But—
every time I'm in the heat
of a huddle. In a gym or
barbershop. When I swig
cold brews & watch
mob flicks by myself—
Rodney, you chase after me.
You kick my ass.
You nail me square
to the ground.

Self-Dialogue Staring at a Mirror

You see yourself in pastels, neatly groomed
Tossing a Frisbee in a college brochure.
Puberty was kind to your pores.
Three Bambi-esque beauty marks
Punctuate your baby face.
What you want is a box cutter's calling card
Stapled to your cheek. Brass knuckle–serrated
Jawlines. Tiny Band-Aids over gashed eyelids.
Most days you wash in the sink, head slumped,
Refusing a smudge-free reflection.
Today you lean hard into that bathroom mirror
& your blank, brown face
Becomes the image of an image, pixilated.
You see a man who pees standing up.

I remember the scene in that movie

when the brown jock uprooted from the Bronx
beats his teacher at literary charades. Flared nose
pointing toward a ceiling, the teacher cants dense
lines of verse, of which the homie always knows the authors.
What you may recall is the kid's Scottish mentor
sauntering into an assembly, squashing plagiarism allegations
and saving the brown jock from expulsion.
You're probably thinking this is about white men.
About gold-encrusted measuring sticks. How in the world
outside that movie, those men could pass for twins. You're right
I was wrong. Their game, like a literary "name that tune."
Guess which dead white dude poet wrote this. Wrong
again. Do you figure a brown jock from the Bronx
could grasp geometry behind an arc or pool cue?
From whom or what does he learn dead white dude poets?
Here I am, stumped about whose brother I be. I think
the teacher was gaming. I think the jock was just playing,
but then, how does one finesse canon?

Some Revisions

for Raleigh Lee

My friend Raleigh always jokes
You must know every black guy
in Bloomington, Indiana
because I break my neck to nod
when one crosses our path, as if
to say: It's good to see myself
for the first time again. As if
to say: It's good to see you.
     Let me start over.
Riding the campus bus with Raleigh
one day, my head lifted from its ledge
and landed at the feet of a mannequin
who peered straight through me.
And that's just what I thought too:
He's a mannequin black man; sitting there
all stiff in his cowboy boots and straight-leg
Levi's. He's a mannequin black man.
Too stilted to acknowledge himself
when he sees me. And by that I meant:
Too stilted to acknowledge me.
     One more time.
So I'm in transit when I see this brotha
across the aisle with his near-brown,
green-eyed son. And just as he looks
at me. No, just as he turns away
a twang or drawl betrays his lips.
He is not speaking to me.
He's talking, smiling at an old white

moth of a woman, well, wasp
if you consider her dilated pupils.
And all of a sudden I pretend
his affliction is not my own.

      This isn't working, is it?
Raleigh. Brother. When you asked
Is it difficult to write about race?
I meant to say Hell yes. Yes.
Especially if you're stilted. Like me.
I find it much safer to sit at home
and feign an understanding. But
to write race is to stare firm. I suppose
you knew that.
You meant *Push me*
to write about race. To re-see.
And I didn't know enough then
to advise you. Well,
I may have learned something
one keystroke ago.

      Race is a triangular maze
of lush green hedges that stretch
beyond the eye's reach.
Black as I am. Yellow as you are.
As neither as this town is,
it has taken a poem: a bus,
tearing through that maze,
full speed in my direction
for me to look at you and nod.
Yes. I meant to say
Write it. And please,
don't stop.

Love Letter to Dave Chappelle

Dear Dave,
Discovery's turned on. I am watching
sheets of ghastly, squirming, horny termites
gnawing inside a wall and missing you.
Today marks my twelfth stab at this.
Each time I begin to say something real
I collapse. Shortcomings. You understand.
This is not the one about the black comedian.
Or his fear of the toddler
pushing Kush on an ave. in the a.m.
This is not about the moment after
that joke. When the audience
slump, just a smidgen, in their seats.
When they question your position
on the ghetto's flowchart
or reconsider a weed dealer's
average age. And when they laugh—
well, this does not concern that.
This isn't a poem
about some cowboy cracking up
over a blackface skit. How his cackle
sounded like a bigot's brain
lodged inside a beating heart, thinking
out loud. This is not about that sound
imploding the logic for your craft.
Not about you leaving me hoarse
and lonely on Wednesday nights.
I repeat. This is not a love thing.
Not even a little.

Jazz Musicians

for Vince, Dean & Josef

The bass player does not matter. Nor
  his right index—plucking
a note so deep dead skin ricochets
  from a fat steel string to a woman's
crystal glass of Grigio. No. It doesn't

matter. The trombone player's lips split
  clench & swell each dark hair
on my left big toe. No matter the alto
  saxophonist's other life. That this
gig saves us both tonight. The banquet hall

is chock-full of entomologists scouring
  the joint for hors d'oeuvres. The room
talks too loud to hear the fat chewed
  between drummer and boy wonder
on the Rhodes. But based on their

clamp-toothed grins, I think swine. Greasy
  tough & filling. Death-driving.
The band's name: Urban Transport.
  Bus systems drive sane men
batty. The wash of blank stares. All those

ant mandibles sculpting sanctuaries
        from sand, inside sidewalk cracks beneath
street signs. Stop. After stop-stagnant. How
        Granddad saw a jazzman's life. In 1962
he made my eighth-grader pops trek 27 blocks

to a dive pawnshop, double bass strapped
        to his back. Claimed it a bad bloodline.
Likely hocked for heroin. Said the future in jazz
        was an early exit to an underground room.
Now my father riffs

most days in the cellar with me, crooning eloquent
        about voting Independent to make
some kind of point. Don't you hear me?
        Entomologists study ants. Even if I think
the world would keep grinding on without them.

Someone should tell this to us who die early.
        A saxophone is called an ax. The horn
is an ax. Ask Jericho. Nothing can stop a song.
        Think chain gang. Or ants whistling
inside cracks. Because they must.

The CEO of Happiness Speaks

Mostly what I do is exercise my lungs
in praise of everything:

Meryl Streep movies. Porcelain
roosters. Daisies. Fuchsia teddy bears

gifted to better halves at carnivals.
Every bike trail and alleyway. Every

single road I walk is lined with the signage
of joy. And I'm not exactly complaining

but imagine being this way full-time.
Compare it to staring at the sun too long—

What happens after.   Goldenrod grid
viewpoint.   World as scatterplot.

My punch clock ticks from the second
I wake and it's hard to tell the difference

between shifts. Think pleasure as computer-
generated dots. Palm trees like pinstripes.

Think I'm crazy if you want
but the world actually moves me maybe

once every year. Last night it happened
at a party, when Jackie told a story

about a kid who couldn't tie her shoes.
Mornings at the tired bus stop. Try

after try, she'd loop and swoop her heart out—
folding in front of peers. But before first bell

in the bathroom stall. Or during gym
in a low-traffic corner,

her best friend, Kim, fashioned her laces
into elegant bows. She did this

with a smile. For years. Imagine
an act selfless as ducking down.

As bending at the knee, away from a crowd.
Some of what I do requires overwatering

in favor of a happy, local clientele.
My job is important, and I like it and all.

But I love that Jackie's story was told
in first person. Think genuflection

with no motive other than praise.
Think of Kim and Jackie making my job

easy but hard. Picture Jackie carefully
sliding off white Keds

to savor Kim's craftsmanship. Envision
those loops. Indefinitely intact.

Now, think of what makes you happy.
Get back to me. We'll do lunch.

Self-Dialogue with Marcus

In every movie there's a snaggletooth thug who pimps broken
speech or a snob poodle who shits for a living named Marcus.

It's like Marcus is the sleepless infant who weeps without fail
while you're tonguing her navel by starlight. Fuck every Marcus.

He's why you sail a hole-punched keel to nowhere you've never been.
Rastas love Garvey. Raised Methodist, died Catholic, ask Marcus

to name a market for his prayers. Miller's no better. His bass
music's fairly funky but he'd write in couplets too. Marcus,

who did this to you? Mr. Schenberg, who says this CK
brief packages right? Why not free-ball? It's gotta be Marcus

meaning Mars, or Ares in Rome. Today you got space suit high
in your underwear to declare self-war. That's just like Marcus

Aurelius penning that progressive, tender self-help text
then stoning 10,000 Christians. Empire was his Marcus

for that. In Marcus, Iowa, there's one market, five large churches
& a kid who can't absolve his bass ax-jones. What's his Marcus

tell me that. You can't tell what's homestead or honed to save your life.
Nights you shrivel through a rib in your yacht's gut. & though Marcus

can rarely swim in film, still, you live to drown another day.
& the Marcus for this Marcus is most certainly Marcus.

Something Like Sleep

Something like sleep dangled our heads from great heights. All of us, snuggling up to book bags and laptops in muddled morning light. A hard halt brought snow-flecked wind and three shadows to our heated bedroom—two of which shot past and rang through opposite sides of the aisle, arms outstretched, slapping what sounded like knees and seats. Something like a lightbulb triggered inside the bus and a fair-haired woman shivered in a dingy pink cardigan near the driver's seat. Her fine jawline was full of life despite two types of red blooming from cheeks—only one of them chapped. Maybe we were all hungover—too taxed from late nights at the office or library to wake. Perhaps, we were in another world—our headphones too jacked to decipher the driver when he rose from his seat, shrugged those monstrous shoulders, and said whatever he said. Seeing this commotion, two tiny blond girls, pigtails peering from wet skullcaps, stomped toward the teary spectacle. Forming a wall before the driver, they spun the woman's knees, nudged her hamstrings into winter wind streams, heads heavy with what pulls at my pen.

I'm a Sad, Sad Man. So Sad

I can't remember how to ride a bus right.
Just the other day, I forgot who I was

and couldn't budge to help a human in need
because the pen in my pocket was poking

my thigh saying, *Use me. Use them. Write
their stories.* As if I am not them—

that woman and her two little girls, mounting
some ten-ton thing daily, fare or no fare

rust bucket but not broken down, traveling
at a pace beyond my control. And how sad

it is, because I'm really not them. Most days
I keep at least a buck in my pocket to pay

the driver and if not, a briefcase, which says
I'm good for it. That was, somehow, miserable

to admit. I'm only telling you this because
you're reading a poem, probably spend

perfectly good bar nights feeling the world
deeply with the ballpoint pen in your pocket

and though a tad abnormal to discuss
all humans want to understand everything

and for everyone to understand us.
What I can't understand is what makes me

see differently, any three people on a bus.
Maybe the saddest thing

in the world, is not knowing how to feel
cold, plastic bus seats without thinking

of narrative arc—the ten thousand pains shifting
uncomfortably from cheek to raw-red cheek

and at any given moment. This.

To You

They were curious.
The twelve baggy black T-shirts
chanting onstage at the local college bar.
Their chorus: *Who's sucking dick, tonight?*
And from the back of the room
where I noted polos and slick dresses
bobbing "yes" to chest-throbbing bass,
every belt crack, backhand, and tongue bash
in me said, *Son, do the right thing*
and stay in your line.
A line I took to mean, Mind your business:
Don't spring the fire alarm.
Don't set the joint ablaze.
Don't rush a live mic
pleading to the baggy black shirts, *Stop.*
Please. There's a spindly raised hand
with chipped red polish quaking too fast
in this smoke-free bar. And a dainty mom
lugging her son piggyback
leveled a letterman to answer your call.
I'm trying to tell you I've been over this
again and again. What type of man would
let a child in this poem? What type of man
could stand in that building and not know
how to be a normal human being?
Could not glean, exigently, something
of addiction, its manic blood-itch?
Comprehend what can happen
when certain little boys in this poem

can do nothing but stay in their lines?
See, I'm doing it again. Damn this
business of frame and context. Dam
these sorry lines and hear me now.
I don't rightly know who sucked off whom
or what variety of human I've become.
But if you don't close this book; I mean
drop this poem straightaway—you, me,
that boy, his mom, and every drunk dancing
fool in this shattered glass-disco-ball world,
we are all of us, altogether fucked.

Nature of the Beast

I cooked us dinner. Now,
you can wash the dishes.
This logic's like
a jolly, wide-framed stockbroker
giving an elderly woman the Heimlich
at a bistro then sneering, *Now*
pick your dentures off the tile and finish
my plate of Brussels sprouts. No, it's like
an aardvark snouting a barefoot kid into
a liquor store, saying, *I sniffed the fire ants*
from your sandbox. Now—about that brew.
Do I have a giant purse full of Geritol?
Am I saying my wife's an anteater? No.
She's vegan. Of course, she would want
you to know she's no linebacker either.
And she's not. But one could say Jill
possesses linebacker-esque attributes
when bolting through our studio door
shoulder first, wearing black leather,
walked-in pumps, tackling her man
by his leg with her tongue. Go ahead
scrutinize. But you should hear how
she tears into me. I'll kiss her brow.
She'll suckle my neck. We'll descend
upon the couch, ankles in my lap as I rub
her feet, and she'll go, *Can you take the dog*
out. I worked all day. And I will
absolutely lose it, because I've been writing
this all day, which is harder than her gig

playing with lab rats. Plus, there's the matter
of grammar. A man who can dismantle
and reerect a world with words can certainly
walk Chauncey, our basset hound, down a flight.
Yes, I actually tell her this. Not that it matters.
Jill may as well be shoving me down
the stairwell when she frowns like I'm shorter
than I am, exclaiming, *Thanks for the help, hun!*
In the courtyard, I watch a portly man
in a petite blazer work his girth free from
a steering wheel and waddle toward the building,
embracing a pack of toilet paper like a life raft.
Chauncey peers at me droopy eyed, slurs the grass,
and we lap the creaky man on our way upstairs.
Hearing the door swing wide, Jill jumps
off the couch to apologize for what she does
not know. I stop her two sentences in.
I kiss her cracked palm, sliding a finger in
my mouth. We nick the dog
when she yanks it out, shoving me groundward.
And we lie there; until the sun joins, then beats us up,
before I nuzzle her awake saying, *Jill. Something*
about what I do has rendered me a bit sensitive:
to transparent reasoning, stockbrokers, people
mixing up ability and desire, competition,
aardvarks. Do you get what I'm saying here?
She looks down at my cheek on her chest, smacks
the top of my head with her lips, and mumbles,
If I could, I really would trade you jobs.
I smile—a little nervous. But mostly, relieved.

Maybe the Saddest Thing

is a shovel sighing earth—
is what's stirring beneath a well,
where I always go: that suck and push
of air, swelling the chest—its starting
place. That I couldn't end there
is as sad and annoying
as watching a pet mouse collide and
collide with its mirrored-glass quarters:
is any ordinary beast acknowledging himself
with a battering ram—dense stump
that slams through the wrong door
in a smoky hallway, reconstructing
the face of an elderly woman
as dumb gold teeth can do.
It's the slim probability of that and
the swinging arm of death falling
for the woman's granddaughter
at the funeral, who has stems as
if a comet's trail could begin at an ankle
and end in a dark, stockinged thigh.
And just like that, we're back:
in the chamber which regulates all.
If you're locked outside its door
or cannot find this room, I sing:
You are lucky as a virgin.
If you're unsure this place exists—

this saddest thing—
Fine. Don't believe in it
or me. But please believe in this
latched dirt-box of a house
speaker strapped to my back, blasting
everything blue—the same.

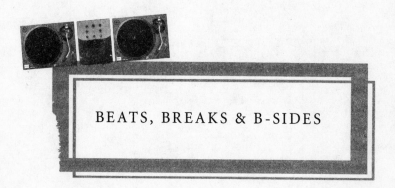

BEATS, BREAKS & B-SIDES

Ars Poetica in the Mode of J-Live

It's like this, Anna:

shell banged bare
with a bat, Anna

vat of gunpowder
shed, Anna

famished bird
fed off scraps, Anna

gut-itch flown
south for life, Anna

dropper's stool self-pecked
slow, Anna

wince or stool
dropped again, Anna

bird sifting
through his shit, Anna

slug built by a bird's
beak, Anna

small handgun.
It's like this, Anna.

Like a gun
the bird doesn't grip.

It's like this, Anna.
It's like that.

It's like that
and like this.

When Keeping It Real Goes Wrong

for Rashad who said

The difference between bad & good
*   rap is the difference between*
silicone & flesh. He legit yelled that

shit through a karaoke mic
        while arranging end caps
on an overnight shift. & I swore

he wasn't lying. Wasn't dropping
        some inverse analysis
about the sad plasticity of pop.

His shopping cart quaked
        as he snatched a glittered
jewel case, like

If we stock one more
*   garbage-ass album, homeboy*
I'ma burn Circuit City to the ground.

What happened next began
        with a black Bic lighter
sparked & lowered to the corner of

a cardboard box. The corners of
        my lips slow-motion switched
from laughter to *Don't do it!*

as he drew an aerosol air spray
        from his slacks. I knocked
the can from his hand but it was too late—

the box burst into a small campfire
        & we stomped out
the wack CDs. It was a long walk

to the restroom. He tented his
        left thumb under the drain, said
Niggas be spending they last

on making good records. Then go
        hungry cause we won't
stock 'em.   Normally

ice in the base of a glass, "Big Brother"
        Shad had lost his cool. Rifling
through his CD wallet he flipped

each page with a silver box cutter.
        I watched him slice open bricks
of blank discs & load up two dozen CPUs.

What was played was circular
        braggadocio. Baritone gusto
about being better than every man

breathing, underrated & hated on. Whole
        songs saying, I've been feeling this
way for eternity. Been

scribbling rhymes since
    my brother passed in '89. &
I spit to box out my rents' chronic

scrapping. & I've suffered more
    than most in a short time
alive so my story's realer than yours.

I wanted to tell our manager
    I stayed for the music. That
I had to hear what fever-inducing

swagger sounded like.
    Needed to watch
Shad line shelves with unkempt

voices. That the store needed it too.
    But surveillance cams
saved me the trouble

of punking out.
    For ten years, I've kept
Shad's voice tucked

just beneath my tongue. & today
    I think he was saying
the important art feels real

talks the talk, and probably
    that's enough. Or
are those my words in his mouth?

All I know
    is that on any given day
there are two types of people, at least:

One who'd go hungry—get fired
    to be heard. & one who'd hide
inside a maze full of lines.

When faced with the statement "there are more black men in jail than college," I think Order of Operations

P.
I think I distrust statisticians.
I think this is problematic.
I think the square root of this quote is a question.
I think the question equals at least five answers.

E.
I think history is the base of most things.
I think the superscript could read 1619.
I think the superscript could be the current year.
I think history is a linear accumulation.

M.
I think if math is wealth then wealth is history.
I think X marks a continent of loss.
I think the more you multiply the more you have.
I think so much depends on personal pronouns.

D.
I think the inverse of history is heritage.
I think heritage halved is power.
I think power has varied degrees.
I'm still thinking personal pronouns.

A.
I think who you are says a lot.
I think the second person implies two sides.
I think it says less plus less equals less.
I think it says more plus more equals more.

S.
I think deducting anything adds a negative sign.
I think the question equals more than five answers.
I think statistics can't fix quotes or crises.
I think this is problematic.

Stakes Is High

. . . 'cause his life is warfare.

—MOS DEF AND TALIB KWELI

You know those people who are uncomfortable
having a conversation at a comfortable level?
Like, you ask Tony his thoughts on Kobe
or the LA Lakers. And Tony responds:
Schwarzenegger ruined their state.
Four years in office and more debt than '03?
Come on, man. Fuck California.
Yeah. So Tony's my dad. He's retired
but doesn't know it. He thinks sleep is
death's first cousin. Early a.m.s
my brother and me tiptoe meandering routes
around our house, avoiding his line of sight.
These are the hours he tunes to AM talk.
Reads his paper where the stakes are high.
Two Decembers ago, my brother Brian and me.
We're sharing cognac sips and cigarillos
shooting stars in a powdered driveway
when dad breaks from the Al Sharpton Hour.
Tracks prints to basement floor. He starts in
on precipitation: *What type of grown-ass men*
trek lines of snow through a house?
Me and your mama raised you better than that.
He shifts into hyperbole: *When you two start*
having kids, I hope you take plenty of movies.
Your mama and me plan to kick back—watch
the decline of common courtesy. Then Brian

makes a wrong move. Smiles. Says snow was
trailed in a square. Technically a half rhombus.
Pops leaves us. Leaves the earth: *Oh, so you*
wanna joke about geometry? I hear scientists
developed a system for tracing racist thoughts.
Can you use your math on that?
Someone should make a drug to kill every last
bigot in the world. They should pump that shit
through the faucets. Drunken laughs march Dad out.
In what world does he live? Michigan bigots
own bunkers. Unregistered land. And if I spent
one summer as a survey worker, if I phoned a woman
named Shanquita and assumed she lived in a hood,
is that intra-racist? Is it double-back racist to assume
you assume she was black? To assume you are not?
Would I be exempt from the ax? Could a black poet
fail the test? Let's say yes. Let's call my F a defect
of private schooling and exclusive subdivisions.
Let's call my death another gulp in the throat
of history's tireless typhoon, spinning backward.

The Light

I caught it like a shard of glass catches a beam.
How a stranger's smile can level a man. Can light

his sunken chest. Swell a new breath. In other words
I was the shard who glinted your eyes. In that light

blue halter, fifth hour, you were the poetry
I normally ignored. Your ballpoint's clean marks. Light

blue, light touch against my windbag essays. That made
you especially stunning. Made you lightening

I had to harness, hand in hand, beneath a desk. Or
in an unattended dark room. Tenderly, red light

washing over us. As I did. Abruptly—telling
you it takes the right type of girl to make a black-white

relationship work. You loved how Common rapped "The Light."
I listened to him more than you. His sly anti–white

woman rhymes never touched me. But you. You filtered through
a magnifying glass. Warmed the cherry orchard, white

with frost. Your light sweetened my pit. You are lightning
crashed through his pulpit into this poem. Beaming. Yes, white.

A gleaming ax hacked through what we were growing into.
I was the ax. You were two syllables too many. White

space in a wheeling sonnet. A corner I couldn't turn
in nine lines. But now I am mourning. Thanks to you, first light.

Bonita Applebum

Do I love you? Do I lust for you?
Am I a sinner because I do the two?
                    —A TRIBE CALLED QUEST

Because you introduced me to Wu-Tang
kung fu flicks, *Five Fingers of Death*
& *36 Chambers*
over quarter candy & sweet peach Faygo
pop on a playground bench.
Because you held my hand
as I cranked the boom box volume knob.

Because you lived next door to my boy B.
Because he slept through twelfth grade
to the tape-recorded husk of your voice.
Because he never graduated
he stayed home & mostly kicked it
with a hustler, turned third-shift grinder.
His name was D. He lived by you too.
B. got fed, turned out cool & normal.

Because I nodded to your chest's thump
under a rocket's trail of smoke
strong enough to trace every porch
couch, box spring & classroom in Kzoo.
Your cherry gloss lingered around
each Olde E bottle I downed.
Because I studied you in college.

I want you to sound bad.

Because you are mine.
Because I refuse to share
let's say you're an overwhelming
total body high.

Because your mouth
is the nectar & squish of a peach.
Because your lips are the color
of a flowering quince.

You ghost-rode your banana-seat
bike through my yard. Miss Bonita,
I caught your bug & couldn't kick it.

Who in their right mind thinks they can put a stop to hip-hop, if it don't stop till I stop, and I don't stop till it stops?

So wrap your cultured-up skull around this. I woke
to a red cross stenciled onto mismatched logs

and "The Entertainer" weeping from a black baby
grand—each note a hound dog's droopy ear. Hear

me when I say, I was lost. Stranded at a teen arts camp
so north in the UP I was hearing southern tongues.

Some flanneled blond man trailed a finger in the air.
Bumped cha head perdy good there. Reckon ya

twisted that ankle on this. He aimed at my foot
with the bottom of a snapper's lacquered shell—

hazy compact, reflecting a dark, faceless me. *Am I
in heaven?* I asked. He cackled at that; shaking his

bronze leather face at the wall, *No, no. 'Least not like him.*
My vision steadied on a hunchback boy in a yellowed white

tee as I rose from the cot. His erratic, thunderous sniffling
spooked words in my throat: *Is he going to be, all right?*

*—Oh yeah. That there's just my little boy, Tim. Been
carryin' on like that since a babe. Just a-cryin' and playin'*

piano that way. Go'on over and say hello.
I joined the boy of five or six at the small black bench

and forced a nervous smile. Timmy's glassy blue eyes
kept time with a wooden metronome. His pupils shrank

and grew. Shrank and grew; dilating on each upbeat.
What if I said he wrapped my hands around his

wrist? Would you think me stoned as Snoop Dogg
at a slain rapper's wake if I told you he stared? That

he wept and played? You think I'm talking shit.
His pupil's penny-size screen flashed small

looped horrors: the snapper's shriveled head
lopped off with a Boy Scout knife; a muscled teen

pissing on an old, vagrant man, drooling snuff
on courthouse steps; the night clerk's nose stud

nailed to a bloody boot heel. You better believe
I bounced; hopped toward an exit. But Timmy

kept on playing, drilling notes into me
like a downpour thumping a well.

True story. The boy never left that room.
Go ahead. You can ask me how I know.

The Message or Public Service Announcement Trailing a Meth Lab Explosion

The edge I'm at is eleven feet high and safer than
the dirt lot below, where shattered glass doubles

as ground. Three rusted-out pickup trucks
have been outfitted with yellow steel boots

and stuffed with flames, igniting steady gusts
of ammonia—bodily and actual—a smell

inextricably related to the tear ducts that also
combusted here, and why I'm standing atop

a single-wide eyeing punched-in mobile home
darkness.   I'm thinking

about Grandmaster Flash. "The Message":
an open row of a freshly set chessboard, bleak

beneath a pink, umbrella-donned table. And
the two rats, fat as badgers, schlepping around

a dog's charred carcass is the move I will make
to hurt you. It's 3 a.m. I just pulled off a Nowhere,

Indiana road to watch a trailer park smoke. A fist
of ash like nail polish scorched with salt blasts

me to my knees. Everything disintegrates
from this angle. Bit by bit. Like blacktop

sweating off layers in sun. Like police tape
singed with flame. From this point of view

soot cloaks stars. Even a white, grinning moon
finds its cheekbones eliminated here. I'm talking

about real lives and white rock rubble. Eyelids,
pocked with reddening cinder. Noses, eroded

and raw. I'm wondering if a face on fire
looks the same in any city. In any hue.

A phone rings an answering machine awake.
The trailing silence hearkens a boarded-up

project building. And in one great big empty
alleyway after another, people are boxed in

or burning up. Vanishing into thin air. Here
I am again, sketch pad in hand, glued to this spot

watching smoke stifle everything—white
and black chess pieces melting in slow mo.

The Chronic

& the mother cops a stiff
    pull from the glass bong.
& murky water gurgling
    in the bulb-like chamber
is barely heard but indistinctly
    audible over Roy Ayers's
interstellar vibe. & smoke clouds
    the bong's fat green neck
& glides down the woman's throat
    into her belly
where it blooms into a beautiful
    exhale.   Toke two
takes the same route
    but springboards
from the gut, splatters
    a brain cell. & in that small
space & for nine sublime songs
    sun trickles into her thoughts.
She thinks about hydroponics. About
    five-gallon buckets & fertilizer.
About thousand-watt sodium vapor
    lights, pruning shears &
the invisible hand. She considers
    the self-regulating nature
of a marketplace. How it's all bullshit
    & doesn't apply to her
life. How her insides are a kind
    of marketplace. She thinks
about supply & demand &

obtrusively marked state lines.
About how people are never this way.
        How our states are so rarely
pronounced. The way we're always
        passing through this & that
in the supermarket or Laundromat &
        without batting an eyelash.
She contemplates clam chowder.
        How it costs a buck
but triggers New England
        Xmas morns, gifts netting
her childhood & the bed
        of a pickup truck—
a man's hand hooking her throat.
        She thinks about dirt roads &
green, green grass. The number
        of yards crossed
to put a ziplocked smile
        in her hands. & it doesn't
matter what's bothering the woman.
        It's heavy. & back in the room
her two little boys are laughing &
        zooming toy cars along carpet
or coiling springy phone cords
        around their necks. & good
or bad those kids are learning something.
        Some states are harder to access
every year. & the mother could just
        as easily be a father. & down
the block & around the corner & in
        double-wides & mansions
this is happening. & these people sit

inches from your cubicle.
They teach in your schools & sing
       in your choir. Make your lattes
& dental appointments. They walk
       your streets & sleep in
your bed. & on & on & on. &
       sometimes these people
are you.

The Break Beat Break

originates from "Break Beat." As in,
the faithful kick drum ride cymbal solo pattern
that never fails to unlock a host of holy ghosts

in any B-boy with a pulse. As in, James Brown.
Anything by James. As in, the "Amen Break"—
six seconds of a liquored-up Gospel B-side.

The break in Break Beat Break comes from you.
It is part of our collective audio unconscious.
A pause for the cause. The cause being the body's

never-ending addiction to movement, which, spun
backward on a turntable, would reveal a link
to thought. It happens on a deserted island

of a song, when a funky-ass fault line rips through
your bass-induced Buddhist empty state and you
start thinking, *Damn. What breed of human am I?*

*What type of man walks around with rhythm rattling
the trunk of his dome?* And wherever you are you run
to the closest piece of light-reflecting glass, say *Oh,*

that's right, I do. You become a drum-dumb addict
and never recover. You let the Break Beat break
into your closet. Headphones on, you nod toward

high-water cords, think *Yeah, that's me.*
My walk alone could make tight pants fit.
You bounce to the bathroom absentminded, brush

teeth with Break Beat Breaks. They start
looking like moldy gold fronts, and you say
Yo, this yellow is classic! An unfilled cavity.

You'd gladly crumble a break into a blunt
wrapper, roll it up, and smoke if you could
keep that mighty Midas-high in your body

for even thirty days. Baby, when the break starts
knocking everything you think turns to music.
And dancing never felt so motherfucking right.

Notes on Beats, Breaks & B-Sides

"Ars Poetica in the Mode of J-Live"
Composed in the mode of J-Live's "It's Like This, Anna."

"When faced with the statement 'there are more black men in jail than college,' I think Order of Operations"
Title remixes the following lines from Showbiz and A.G.'s "Runaway Slave." "Nine out of ten are black on black crimes / Four out of nine were killed before their prime / The other five wanted vengeance / So now five out of five are doing a jail sentence."

"Stakes Is High"
Title samples De La Soul's "Stakes Is High." Epigraph samples Black Star's "Astronomy (8th Light)."

"The Light"
Title samples Common's "The Light." Poem alludes to lines from Common's "Hungry." "Downtown interracial lovers hold hands / I breathe heavy like an old man with a cold can of Old Style."

"Bonita Applebum"
Title and epigraph sampled from A Tribe Called Quest's "Bonita Applebum."

"Who in their right mind thinks they can put a stop to hip-hop, if it don't stop till I stop, and I don't stop till it stops?"
Title samples J-Live's "Longevity."

"The Message or Public Service Announcement Trailing a Meth Lab Explosion"
Title samples Grandmaster Flash and the Furious Five's "The Message."

"The Chronic"
Title samples Dr. Dre's *The Chronic*.

Acknowledgments

Thanks to the editors of the following journals where these poems appeared, sometimes in earlier forms:

Anti- / "The Break Beat Break," "Self-Dialogue with Marcus"

Beloit Poetry Journal / "Maybe the Saddest Thing," "The Message or Public Service Announcement Trailing a Meth Lab Explosion," "Who in their right mind thinks they can put a stop to hip-hop, if it don't stop til I stop, and I don't stop til it stops?"

Boston Review (Online) / "Stakes Is High"

Cave Canem XIII / "To You"

The Collagist / "The CEO of Happiness Speaks," "To You"

Columbia Poetry Review / "Love Letter to Dave Chappelle"

Crab Orchard Review / "Some Revisions"

cream city review / "Love Letter to Bruce Leroy"

DIAGRAM / "Ars Poetica in the Mode of J-Live"

Harpur Palate / "Love Letter to RuPaul"

Hayden's Ferry Review / "Everything I Know About Jazz I Learned from Kenny G"

jubilat / "Love Letter to Justin Timberlake," "Self-Dialogue Watching Richard Pryor Live on the Sunset Strip"

Minnesota Review / "I'm a Sad, Sad Man. So Sad"

Missouri Review (Online) / "Love Letter to Flavor Flav"

Muzzle / "Love Letter to Pam Grier"

Mythium / "Self-Dialogue Camping at Yellowwood State Forest," "When faced with the statement 'there are more black men in jail than college,' I think Order of Operations"

PANK / "About the Time Two Ducks Advised Me on Matters of the Flesh," "Oblivious Spring"

Southern Indiana Review / "1998," "Interrupting Aubade Ending in
    Epiphany," "Self-Dialogue Staring at a Mirror"
Sou'wester / "Love Letter to Jim Kelly"
Vinyl Poetry / "I remember the scene in that movie," "The Light,"
    "Something Like Sleep."

Many thanks to D. A. Powell for selecting this book for the
National Poetry Series and for his sincere, thoughtful support.

Thanks to the National Poetry Series and HarperCollins Publish-
ers for the gift of a book. Special thanks to Michael Signorelli at
Harper Perennial for his eternal patience and editorial expertise.

I owe a tremendous debt to all my teachers, especially Maurice
Manning, Ross Gay, and Romayne Rubinas Dorsey. Their incred-
ible, generous teaching opened up a world for me.
Nothing but love to my friends and colleagues at Indiana Uni-
versity.

Endless thanks to the Fine Arts Work Center; for the time and
space; for the sea; for the beautiful people you placed in my life.
For the love and support, much gratitude to Cave Canem, where
many of these poems began.

I am grateful to the following teachers and friends for comment-
ing on this book or its poems at various stages of development:
Cornelius Eady, Toi Derricotte, Ed Roberson, Maura Stanton,
Claudia Rankine, Colleen McElroy, Rebecca Gayle Howell, Jacob
Shores-Arguello, Myron Michael Hardy, Douglas Brown, and
Cheri Johnson. Thanks to francine harris for allowing me to bor-
row her title "I remember the scene in that movie."

Thanks to William Paine, DeAntae Prince, Chad Anderson, Mike Rowe, and Ashley Rutter for holding me down.

Thanks to Ryan Teitman.

Thanks to Raleigh Lee and Kelly Wilson.

Thanks to Jeff Kass for the spark; to Jason Olsen for the push.

Above all, thank you to my parents and family. This book is theirs.

Marcus Wicker's poems have appeared in *Poetry*, *jubilat*, *Third Coast*, *Ninth Letter*, and *Crab Orchard Review*, among other journals. The recipient of a 2011 Ruth Lilly Fellowship, he has also held fellowships from Cave Canem, the Fine Arts Work Center, and Indiana University, where he received his MFA. Marcus is assistant professor of English at the University of Southern Indiana.